FERDINAND KÜCHLER

CONCERTINO

im Stil von Antonio Vivaldi

D-Dur / D major

für Violine und Klavier / for Violin and Piano

Opus 15

Schülerkonzert (1. und 3. Lage) / Easy Concerto (1st and 3rd position)

Herausgegeben von / Edited by

Franziska Matz

C. F. PETERS

FRANKFURT/M. · LEIPZIG · LONDON · NEW YORK

6-25

Concertino

im Stil von Antonio Vivaldi
D-Dur / D major
für Violine und Klavier
(„Schülerkonzert" 1. und 3. Lage)

I

Ferdinand Küchler (1867–1937)
Op. 15
Herausgegeben von Franziska Matz

Edition Peters Nr. 11029

32553

4

II

Siciliano

III

Nachwort

Ferdinand Küchler (1867–1937) wirkte als Geiger und Geigen-pädagoge viele Jahre in Frankfurt am Main und Leipzig und trat publizistisch in verschiedenen musikalischen Bereichen in Erscheinung,[1] hauptsächlich jedoch durch methodische Werke wie seine *Praktische Violinschule* (2 Bände, 1911). Als Komponist stellte er sich ebenfalls in den Dienst der Pädagogik und verfasste mehrere instruktive Stücke, von denen die meisten als „Concertino" (für Violine und Klavier) betitelt sind.

Innerhalb dieser Werkreihe Küchlers ist das vorliegende *Concertino im Stil von Antonio Vivaldi* op. 15 eine der kürzesten Kompositionen. Der Einleitungssatz (Allegro moderato) knüpft mit seinem Themenmotiv zu Beginn (Auftakt, Quartsprung und 5-fach wiederholter Grundton) an Vivaldis berühmtes a-Moll-Konzert op. 3 Nr. 6 an,[2] zu dem es spieltechnisch die ideale Vorstufe bildet. Vor allem zum Erlernen eines kräftigen Détaché-Strichs und für das Tonleiterspiel in der 3. Lage ist dieser erste Satz hilfreich und anregend.

Das *Siciliano* (Larghetto) klingt wunderschön, selbst wenn der Schüler noch kein Vibrato beherrscht. Voraussetzung ist allerdings, dass ein klarer Bogenkontakt besteht. Außerdem bietet dieser Satz in seiner Kürze eine gute Gelegenheit, elementare Grundlagen der Harmonielehre einzuführen: Nach Tonika und Domiante lernt man z. B. in Takt 11 den „Neapolitaner" kennen. Gerade für Geiger ist es wichtig, sich früh darin zu schulen, die Harmonien unter der gespielten Melodie bewusst mitzuhören.

Der tänzerische Schlusssatz (Allegro assai) im 3/8-Takt ist quasi die Belohnung für die Arbeit am 1. Satz, denn die zuvor erworbenen Fertigkeiten zahlen sich nun bei den kurzen, schwingenden Détaché-Strichen und den 16tel-Läufen mit Lagenwechsel aus. Neu hinzu kommt in den Takten 77–84 die Bogentechnik des schnellen Wechsels über zwei benachbarte Saiten. Da diese Spieltechnik in der Violinliteratur aller Epochen anzutreffen ist, kann der Schüler nicht früh genug beginnen, die lockere, schnelle Kreisbewegung von Hand und Arm zu trainieren.

In der Ausgabe gibt die Violinstimme über dem Klavier den Notentext in der Lesart der ersten Druckausgabe wieder; die separate Violinstimme hingegen enthält die spieltechnische Einrichtung der Herausgeberin. Im Klavierpart wurden aus klanglichen Gründen einige zusätzliche („Füll-")Töne vorgeschlagen, die durch Kleindruck kenntlich sind.

Franziska Matz

---

[1] Von Küchlers breitgefächertem publizistischem Wirken zeugen – neben seinen pädagogischen Arbeiten für die Violine – eine *Chorgesangschule* (1915) und eine Abhandlung zu *Goethes Musikverständnis* (1935).

[2] Das Werk wurde von Küchler im Unterricht oft verwendet und sogar selbst ediert: Antonio Vivaldi: *Konzert a-Moll* op. 3 Nr. 6 (Sechstes Konzert aus *L'estro armonico*, RV 356), Edition Peters Nr. 3794.

Afterword

Ferdinand Küchler (1867–1937) was a violinist and violin teacher for many years in Frankfurt am Main and Leipzig. He also appeared in print in a number of musical fields,[1] though chiefly with violin tutors such as his two-volume *Praktische Violinschule* (1911). As a composer he primarily served the interests of learners and wrote a number of instructive pieces, most of which are entitled *Concertino* (for violin and piano).

Küchler's *Concertino in the Style of Antonio Vivaldi*, op. 15, is one of the shortest works in his concertino series. The first movement (Allegro moderato) opens with a thematic motif consisting of an upbeat, a leap of a fourth, and a five-fold repetition of the tonic pitch. In this sense it obviously draws on Vivaldi's famous *A-minor Concerto*, op. 3, no. 6,[2] for which it forms an ideal technical preparation. This movement is especially helpful and stimulating for acquiring a strong *détaché* bowstroke and for playing scalar passages in the third position.

The *Siciliano* (Larghetto) sounds lovely even if the learner has not yet mastered vibrato. The prerequisite, however, is a clear contact with the bow. This short movement also provides a good opportunity to introduce some basic principles of harmony: besides the tonic and dominant, the student can became acquainted with, for example, the "Neapolitan sixth" in bar 11. It is especially important for violinists to be trained at an early age to hear the harmonies beneath the melodies they play.

The buoyant finale (Allegro assai) in 3/8 meter is what one might call a reward for the student's work on the opening movement, for the skills learned there now pay off in short, lilting *détaché* bowstrokes and sixteen-note runs with changes of position. A new technique, the rapid change across two adjacent strings, appears in bars 77 to 84. As this technique is found in the violin literature of every era, learners cannot begin early enough to train a smooth, quick, circular motion of the hand and arm.

In our edition, the violin part printed above the piano accompaniment reproduces the text from the first printed edition. The separate violin part, in contrast, contains performance markings from the editor. A few additional "filler notes," indicated by small print, are suggested in the piano part to enrich the sonority.

Franziska Matz

---

[1] In addition to his educational works for the violin, Küchler's wide-ranging publications include a tutor for choral singing (*Chorgesang-schule*, 1915) and a treatise on Goethe's understanding of music (*Goethes Musikverständnis*, 1935).

[2] This work, the sixth concerto in Vivaldi's *L'estro armonico* (RV 356), was often used by Küchler in his lessons. He even produced an edition of it: *Antonio Vivaldi, Konzert a-Moll op. 3 Nr. 6* (Edition Peters No. 3794).